BRIGHT IDEA BOOKS

THE SEARCH FOR
Alien Life

by Ryan Gale

CAPSTONE PRESS
a capstone imprint

Bright Idea Books are published by Capstone Press
1710 Roe Crest Drive, North Mankato, Minnesota 56003
www.mycapstone.com

Library of Congress Cataloging-in-Publication Data
Names: Gale, Ryan, author.
Title: Search for alien life / by Ryan Gale.
Description: North Mankato, Minnesota: Capstone Press, [2020] | Series:
    Aliens | Includes bibliographical references and index. | Audience: Grade
    4 to 6.
Identifiers: LCCN 2018058403 (print) | LCCN 2018061247 (ebook) |
ISBN 9781543571165 (ebook pdf) | ISBN 9781543571080 (hardcover) | ISBN 9781543574951 (pbk.)
Subjects: LCSH: Extraterrestrial beings--Juvenile literature.
Classification: LCC QB54 (ebook) | LCC QB54 .G24 2020 (print) | DDC 999--dc23
LC record available at https://lccn.loc.gov/2018058403

All internet sites appearing in back matter were available and accurate when this book was sent
to press.

Editorial Credits
Editor: Claire Vanden Branden
Designer: Becky Daum
Production Specialist: Ryan Gale

Photo Credits
iStockphoto: CHBD, 5, manjik, 6–7, Pgiam, cover, sanjeri, 12–13, shanecotee, 19, TerryHealy,
9; NASA: JPL, 11, JSC/Stanford University, 22–23; Shutterstock Images: Antares_StarExplorer,
25, Design Projects, 20–21, gary yim, 16–17, Gorodenkoff, 26–27, PhotoChur, 14–15, 28,
tmcphotos, 31

Design Elements: Shutterstock Images, Red Line Editorial

Printed in the United States   5331

TABLE OF CONTENTS

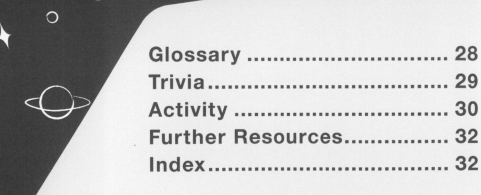

CHAPTER 1

ARE WE ALONE?

People have long wondered if there is life beyond Earth. Some people think **aliens** are real. Others think Earth is the only place with life. People search for life outside this world.

There could be more than 60 billion planets that support alien life in outer space.

Sir William Herschel was a scientist. He used a **telescope** to look into space. He looked at Mars in 1784. He saw dark and light spots. He thought the dark spots were water. He guessed light spots were land.

Planets need water to have life. Herschel thought there could be life on Mars. Scientists later found his findings to be untrue. But he made people want to know more about life in space.

Scientists study Mars because it is close to Earth.

SIR WILLIAM HERSCHEL

Sir William Herschel built many telescopes. He used one to discover the planet Uranus in 1781. He believed there was life on many other planets.

CHAPTER 2

THE SEARCH FOR
Alien Life

People need **proof** to know if aliens are real. One way to find them is to look. People use telescopes to look in space. But telescopes cannot see life far away. They are not strong enough. So people need to get closer.

People began sending rockets into space in the 1950s. Soon they sent spacecraft to other planets. These spacecraft took pictures. They sent them back to Earth. The pictures did not show any signs of life.

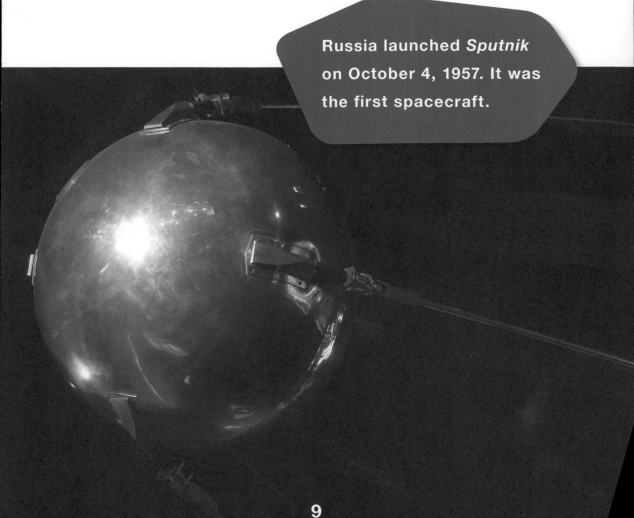

Russia launched *Sputnik* on October 4, 1957. It was the first spacecraft.

The *Pathfinder* reached Mars in 1997. This **satellite** dropped a robot. The robot took pictures. The land looked like a desert. The robot tested the dirt and rocks. There were no signs of life.

NOT TOO HOT OR COLD

Not all planets can have life. Those close to a sun are too hot for life. Those far away are too cold. The space between is the best place for life.

Scientists are still looking for life on Mars. They are also looking on planets farther away.

Pathfinder captured a photo of a rover on Mars in 1997. Rovers are space vehicles that explore other planets.

LISTENING FOR ALIENS

Another way to find aliens is to listen.

Some aliens might use radio signals.

The signals travel through space.

People on Earth can receive them

through **antennas**.

Scientists receive radio signals through antennas. The data goes into a computer.

13

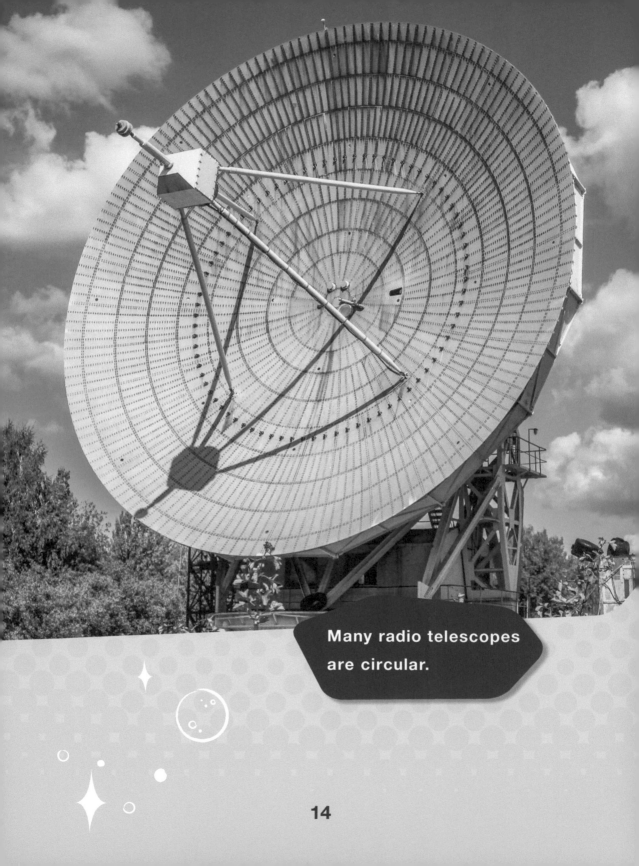

Many radio telescopes are circular.

Frank Drake is a scientist. He looks for life in space. He used a radio telescope in 1960. He listened for aliens. He did not hear any. But he kept looking. Other scientists began listening too. They built bigger radio telescopes.

The Very Large Array is a radio telescope facility in San Agustin, New Mexico.

Today there are radio telescopes all over the world. The biggest is in China. It is as big as 30 football fields. Some are small. They can fit in your backyard.

CHAPTER 3

ALIENS ON Earth

Aliens may have visited Earth. People have seen weird flying objects in the sky. They could be spaceships.

Some people see streaks of light in the sky that they can't explain. They think these streaks could be alien spaceships.

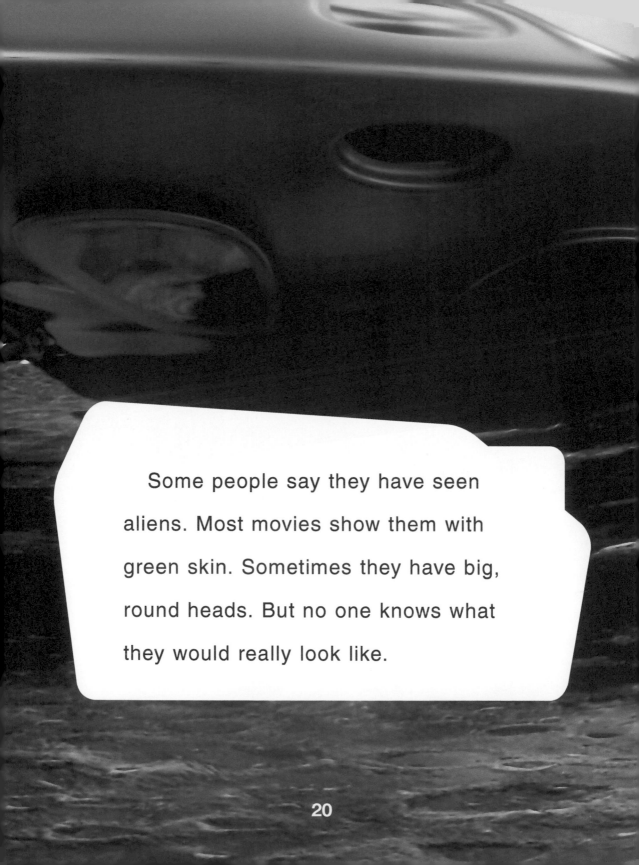

Some people say they have seen aliens. Most movies show them with green skin. Sometimes they have big, round heads. But no one knows what they would really look like.

Many movies show aliens with large heads and yellow-green skin.

21

Some alien life may be too small to see. Rocks from other planets have landed on Earth. Scientists found a rock in 1984. They think it is from Mars. They think they found very tiny **bacteria** on it.

The rock from Mars is 4.5 billion years old.

WHERE ARE the Aliens?

Frank Drake came up with an **equation**. There are many planets in our **galaxy**. The equation guesses the ones that could have life. The number was in the millions.

Our galaxy is one of many. So why is proof of aliens so hard to find?

Earth is in the
Milky Way galaxy.

There could be many reasons we have not found aliens. They may not be real. They may not be able to speak with us. They may be too far away. People may not have the right tools to find them.

The search has been hard. But scientists continue to look for life in space.

Astronauts will continue to help with the search for alien life in the future.

CLOSEST PLANET

The closest planet that could have life is very far away. It is 25 trillion miles (40 trillion kilometers) from Earth. It would take more than 54,000 years to fly there.

GLOSSARY

alien
a creature not from Earth

antenna
a metal rod that receives
radio waves

bacteria
a type of biological cell that
can be a form of life

equation
a mathematic problem

galaxy
a large group of stars and
planets in the universe

planet
a large body that revolves
around a sun

proof
the facts showing that
something is true

satellite
a spacecraft that circles
a larger object in space;
satellites gather and send
information

telescope
an object that is used to look
at things very far away

TRIVIA

1. The Search for Extraterrestrial Intelligence (SETI) Institute is based in California. This organization's mission is to find life on other planets.

2. According to a study done by 20th Century Fox Home Entertainment, nearly one-half of Americans believe aliens have visited Earth.

3. The *Pioneer 10* and *Pioneer 11* went to deep space. They have maps on them. The maps could show aliens how to find Earth.

ACTIVITY

WHAT DO ALIENS LOOK LIKE?

Humans can only guess what aliens look like. Most people think they look close to humans because that is all we have to go on. However, aliens can look completely different from us! Some could be as small as a microbe. Others could look like reptiles. What aliens look like could also depend on the planet they live on. Aliens could look different depending on if they lived on a desert, jungle, or ice planet.

Draw your own planet using paper and colored pencils or markers. Then draw an alien you think could live on your planet. Present your drawing to your friends or family.

FURTHER RESOURCES

Interested in finding out more about aliens and space? Learn more with these resources:

Aguilar, David A. *Alien Worlds: Your Guide to Extraterrestrial Life.* Washington, D.C.: National Geographic, 2013.

Space! New York: DK Publishing, 2015.

Want to learn more about Mars? Check out these resources:

Aldrin, Buzz. *Welcome to Mars: Making a Home on the Red Planet.* Washington, D.C.: National Geographic, 2015.

NASA: Mars for Kids
https://mars.nasa.gov/participate/funzone

INDEX